A Man's Guide To Child Custody

Books by David T. Pisarra, Esq.

A Man's Guide To Divorce Strategy

A Man's Guide to Child Custody

A Man's Guide to Domestic Violence

David T. Pisarra, Esq.

A Man's Guide To Child Custody

Copyright © 2010 by David T. Pisarra

LIBERO MEDIA
1305 Pico Blvd
Santa Monica, CA 90405

All rights reserved. No part of this publication may be reproduced, stored in a retrieval system, or transmitted, in any form or by any means, electronic, mechanical, photocopying, recording, or otherwise, without the prior permission of the publisher.

ISBN: 978-0-9831635-1-0

The information contained in this book is designed to give an overview and is not a substitute for meeting with a competent family law attorney who can review the full set of facts in any particular case. No warranty is made, express or implied and neither Libero Media nor David T. Pisarra assume any liability in connection with any use or result from reliance on the information contained in this book.

"BECAUSE FATHERHOOD IS FOREVER."

This book is written to empower men to know what their legal rights and responsibilities are. So often I find men have no real idea of what is expected from them, and more importantly, what THEY can expect from the legal system.

As a voice for men, I strive to be

direct, honest, and **clear.**

David T. Pisarra, Esq.

A Man's Guide to Child Custody

CONTENTS

TWO QUESTIONS EVERY MAN ASKS 1

CHILD SUPPORT IN A NUTSHELL 3

CHILD SUPPORT FAQS 2

1) WILL I LOSE MY KIDS?   2
2) WHY DOESN'T SHE HAVE TO ACCOUNT FOR THE CHILD SUPPORT I PAY?   3

CHAPTER 2 – CHILD CUSTODY STRATEGY ISSUES ... 4

DOMESTIC VIOLENCE	5
RESTRAINING ORDERS	6
THE REASON FOR TRO'S IN CUSTODY BATTLES	9
WHY FATHERS NEED TO FIGHT THEM.	10
TROS ARE FOR MEN ALSO! WOMEN ALSO COMMIT BATTERY.	10
FALSE CHARGES OF DOMESTIC ABUSE	11
PITFALLS OF DO-IT-YOURSELF RESTRAINING ORDERS	13

CHAPTER 3 – CUSTODY EXPLAINED 16

LEGAL CUSTODY	16
PHYSICAL CUSTODY	17
VISITATION	19
PATERNITY DEFINED	20
RIGHTS OF UNMARRIED PARENTS	21
SUPERVISED VISITATION	24
CHILDREN OF DOMESTIC PARTNERSHIPS	25

A Man's Guide to Child Custody

CHILDREN'S PREFERENCES IN CUSTODY DISPUTES	26
CREATIVE CHILD CUSTODY AGREEMENTS	27
DETAILS ON VISITATION	27
DEVELOPING A CUSTODY PLAN	28
SPECIAL NEEDS CHILDREN	29
730 EVALUATIONS OF CUSTODY	30
OUT-OF-STATE CUSTODY PROCEEDINGS	32
PARENTAL ALIENATION	33
STEPPED-UP VISITATION	35
UNDERSTANDING CHILD CUSTODY LAWS	36
UNIFORM CHILD CUSTODY JURISDICTION ACT	38
PARENTING PLANS	39
MOVE-AWAY ORDERS	40
MOVE-AWAY OR RELOCATION SITUATIONS	41

CHAPTER 4 - CHILD SUPPORT STRATEGY 44

UNDERPERFORMING AT WORK	44
VOCATIONAL TESTING	46
CHILD SUPPORT	47
CHILD SUPPORT DEFENSE	49
CHILD SUPPORT ENFORCEMENT – FAGE GARNISHMENTS	50
CHILD SUPPORT GUIDELINES	52
CHILD SUPPORT MODIFICATIONS	53
DEPARTMENT OF CHILD SUPPORT SERVICES	53
DISSOMASTER CHILD SUPPORT CALCULATOR	54
HIGH-EARNER CHILD SUPPORT	55
HOW TO CALCULATE A CHILD SUPPORT	56
NEW MATE INCOME	57

CHAPTER 5 – CASE STUDIES 58

A Man's Guide to Child Custody

CHAPTER 6 ESSAYS FOR FATHERS............................. 66

THE THREE P's OF CHILD CUSTODY FOR FATHERS	68
FATHERS SHOULD NOT LEAVE FAMILY HOME	76
FATHER'S DAY SPECIAL: ON FATHERHOOD AND RAISING MEN	82
FATHERS SHOULD GET AN AUTOMATIC 50% CHILD CUSTODY	88

ABOUT THE AUTHOR... 94

A Man's Guide to Child Custody

A Man's Guide to Child Custody

Chapter 1 – The Basics

Two Questions Every Man Asks

Every man wants to know two things.

1) What's it going to cost me? And

2) How long will it take?

Usually men mean, "How much am I going to pay in fees, alimony, child support." The cost of the attorney will be determined largely by your ex and her attorney, you have to accept that part of the process of divorce is being angry. Frequently spouses fight with each other, through their attorneys, not based on logically well thought out reasons, but to express the anger over the breakup.

This is one of the ways that unscrupulous

A Man's Guide to Child Custody

attorneys take advantage of the situation. They crank up the anger and resentment, knowing that it will result in more money being spent on court appearances, depositions, unending document production demands, forensic accountants, psychologists, parenting coaches and the list goes on.

Alimony and Child Support are based on your income. The general rule is that your soon to be ex-wife is entitled to maintain the lifestyle that you have built for her, same goes for the kids. They are entitled to live in essentially equal environments. That's so they don't play favorites, but it can be used by an unscrupulous ex to increase your child support.

The answer to the second question is also dependent on the answer to the first, the more there is at stake, the longer it can take for a

A Man's Guide to Child Custody

divorce to be processed. The actual legal requirements range from a few days to six months. But until the parties are done fighting, it will not end.

Child Support in a Nutshell

Men need to remember that the decisions they make today will have long term effects on their financial well-being many years into the future – this is why an attorney who can see beyond the battle of today is so vitally important to someone going through the fog of a divorce.

When it comes to Child Support, it's a hot issue for men. They have to pay, but have no control over how it is spent - that is a constant source of complaint for men. Mom uses "my kid's money" for her nails, her hair, or her yoga. Well, sorry bout that, but there's

A Man's Guide to Child Custody

nothing you can do. So with that in mind, here are three things you CAN do:

1) PAY BY CHECK – Checks are important because they give you a permanent record of what has been paid. Cash, and Money Orders are easily forgotten about, lost, and don't have a paper trail. Keep your old, cancelled checks until you have a signed release from the mom that you have paid all of your child support, and I mean ALL.

2) BE CLEAR IN YOUR AGREEMENT WHAT YOU PAY FOR – The court will make you pay support, because it goes for things like food, utilities, clothes, but you need to be clear on what you must pay for "In Addition" to the child support.

3) ACCEPT THAT YOU MUST PAY IT – You don't have a choice over how it is spent, it

A Man's Guide to Child Custody

is mom's to do with as she needs. You're better off just making sure you pay it on time, keep a record and forget about it. If your kid needs something, and mom's not buying it, man up and do it yourself without complaint.

A Man's Guide to Child Custody

A Man's Guide to Child Custody

Child Support FAQs

1) Will I lose my kids if I don't pay?
Probably not, but you need to remember that mom will use it against you in a psychological war against you with the kids.

Being broke is not a crime and it can't be used against you in court when it comes to custody. There are two types of custody that we talk about - Legal and Physical.

Legal custody has to do with your right to see your children and make decisions about them. This is difficult to lose, you have to be a pretty bad parent and your ex has to fight you on it.

Physical custody is where they actually

A Man's Guide to Child Custody

live and sleep. Again it is hard to lose ALL physical custody, usually one parent has "Primary Custody" which means the children spend most of their time at that parent's home, and the other parent has visitation.

2) Why doesn't she have to account for the child support I pay?

The court assumes that a custodial parent will use the child support paid, for the maintenance and care of the child. This includes things like rent, food, utilities, and clothing. The court wants to make sure that children are supported in an appropriate manner, that's why they make sure that you pay it, not that she spends it on them in a way that you agree with.

Chapter 2 – Child Custody Strategy Issues

The basic rule on Child Custody is where the children first live, is where they are going to live. This is where many men lose the battle from the get go, if they leave the family home and the children behind, that's where the children are going to be.

Many women like to make sure that dads have as little right to Child Custody as possible, and they ensure that they will have the freedom to do as they please, by starting the battle with a restraining order. The restraining order will have a lasting effect on any future child custody battles.

A Man's Guide to Child Custody

Domestic Violence

Domestic Violence is a tragedy. It is painful, shameful, and psychologically damaging to everyone in the household, especially children who are frequently the innocent observers.

Domestic Violence happens when one person physically attacks another, threatens, harasses, or intentionally disturbs the peace and serenity of the other party.

The true rate of domestic violence is hard to quantify as so many incidents of domestic violence, or spouse on spouse abuse, go unreported. Men are chronic under-reporters of being abused, for fear of being mocked.

There is a social perception that it is okay for a woman to hit a man, and thathe is supposed to just accept it. That is NOT however

A Man's Guide to Child Custody

the law. A man has just as much right, and perhaps more of an obligation, to call the police and have them arrest the perpetrator if he is attacked by his spouse, whether it be his wife, girlfriend, husband or boyfriend.

Anyone who is a victim of Domestic Violence should obtain restraining orders immediately. Men in particular should be aware of how to obtain TROs, and how important they are in a custody battle over children, as they can and will have a dramatic and long term effect on the rights and availability of visitation.

Restraining Orders

Restraining Orders can be obtained in emergency situations by the police when the court system is unavailable. These are called "Emergency Protective Orders" and they are issued by a judge who is "on call" and available

A Man's Guide to Child Custody

to the police, after court hours, over weekends and on holidays.

The more common way to obtain a restraining order is to file a petition under the Domestic Violence Protection Act (DVPA) which is a form that is free to file, asking the court to restrain a person based on the declaration of the victim. The form requires that a person sign a Declaration under PENALTY OF PERJURY stating the grounds for the issuance of an immediate restraining order. People frequently lie on these declarations in order to get immediate custody of the home, children and pets. The first restraining order issued is called a Temporary Restraining Order, and is issued without the court taking actual testimony, and usually the restrained person is not present.

In divorce proceedings these are

A Man's Guide to Child Custody

frequently used to "kick out" one spouse from the home, based on allegations that domestic abuse is occurring. They can be used to require someone to turn in their handguns, stay away from a business they've built, and frequently prevent them from seeing their children.

In California once a person has been kicked out of their home based on a Temporary Restraining Order, a hearing will be set approximately 20 days later for a full hearing on the merits of the initial order. These hearings can last from 5 minutes to days. They should NOT BE IGNORED.

If you have a Temporary Restraining Order against you, seek legal counsel immediately as the hearing is only a few days away and you need to defend yourself against any baseless charges.

A Man's Guide to Child Custody

The Reason for TRO's in Custody Battles

In Child Custody battles, whether as part of a marital dissolution or paternity case, TROs are frequently used to "kick out" one spouse from the home, and to gain custody of the children, based on allegations that domestic abuse is occurring.

If a person is determined to be a Domestic Violence Abuser, which can be based on a statement as simple as "He scared me", they can lose Physical Custody of their children. The "victim" will be granted Primary Physical Custody of the children and that will affect visitation, and more importantly, it makes it extremely easy for the "victim" to move to another city or state if they want to, in order to frustrate your ability to see the children.

A Man's Guide to Child Custody

Why Fathers Need to Fight Them

Once declared an abuser, the presumptions of equal parenting are destroyed. An abuser is considered to be a detriment to the health and well-being of the children and will have to go through a rehabilitation program to comply with court orders, such as anger management classes, parenting classes, and in many cases a 52-week batterer's intervention program.

TROs are for MEN also! Women also commit battery

Men are placed in a terrible position in our society, they are told they cannot hit a woman, but it is okay for a woman to hit a man. Men are told it is "unmanly" to call the police to "fight your fight" against a woman. Frequently an angry woman will call a man a coward if he

A Man's Guide to Child Custody

attempts to call the police, and an abuser if he defends himself.

The answer is that a man MUST CALL THE POLICE if he is being abused. It is not a matter of being called a coward, a wimp, a pussy, a fag or a loser. It is the only way he has a chance of winning. If he can prove that he was not the aggressor, which he can do if he is the one who calls the police first, then he has an argument to the judge in court. If he does nothing, he's going to lose. Any woman that is willing to hit a man, and call him a coward, a pussy, a fag, or a loser, will not think twice about committing perjury to win in court.

False Charges of Domestic Abuse

Domestic abuse and domestic violence are the same thing. False charges of domestic abuse or violence are common and in cases

A Man's Guide to Child Custody

where there are no children, a restraining order will be issued and the couple will separate and go on their way. In families with children, the use of false claims of domestic abuse are used as a means to gain an advantage in child custody fights.

Because a "victim" has such an advantage in court over an "abuser" in a child custody case, there is a strong motive for false charges to be put forth in court. If someone wants to gain custody of the children at all costs, they will not think twice about committing perjury.

This is why if you have been served with a restraining order you need to hire a lawyer immediately to defend yourself.

A Man's Guide to Child Custody

Pitfalls of Do-It-Yourself Restraining Orders

A restraining order can be issued on a declaration signed under penalty of perjury, but the judicial officer who issues the initial restraining order, (one that can kick a person out of their home and prevent them from seeing their children) almost never takes testimony for the alleged victim. Most of the time the "abuser" is not present or even aware that a restraining order is being asked for.

In asking for a restraining order that you have written yourself, you may not ask for enough protection, or you may put statements in your declaration that can be used against you at the hearing on the permanent restraining order. This is why you should always seek the assistance of an attorney who is experienced in preparing restraining orders.

A Man's Guide to Child Custody

Defending yourself against a restraining order is a highly technical skill, and one that requires a lawyer who knows their way around a courtroom, the rules of evidence, and how to get to the truth of a case. Defending a restraining order that is based on lies is extremely difficult and is not something that an inexperienced person should attempt.

A Man's Guide to Child Custody

Chapter 3 – Custody Explained

Legal Custody

Legal Custody is the concept of what rights you have in making decisions for your children's life, and in knowing what is going in their life. Legal custody means being able to see school records, medical records, choosing which school they will go to, and giving consent for medical treatment.

Legal Custody also means the ability to get a passport and travel with the children.

Usually both parents share Legal Custody

A Man's Guide to Child Custody

as a natural part of being a parent. If you are listed on the birth certificate, you would normally automatically have Legal Custody.

To lose Legal Custody, a court must make a ruling that it is not in the best interests of the child for you to have a contributing voice in their upbringing. This is not something that courts do without a large amount of proof that a parent would be a detriment to the child's life. Frequently the loss of legal custody is a consequence of alcohol or drug abuse, sexual abuse, domestic violence, or abandonment.

Physical Custody

Physical Custody means having the children with you when you travel, having them sleep over at your house, feeding, and clothing them.

A Man's Guide to Child Custody

Physical Custody is very much a matter of practicality and logistics. This is the reason that so many fathers do not share equally in the division of physical custody. It is simply not practical for many different reasons, the most common of which is the fact that a father has a job that interferes with his ability to be present for his child.

It is the trap that men are caught in, they are expected to be a good provider during a marriage, and that means they have to work a lot. When the marriage ends, they are expected to continue to provide, but that means that they don't have the time to spend with the children, to shuttle them to soccer games, girl scouts, and all of their activities. Many fathers would gladly give up working so hard to have more time, but they are now legally bound to provide alimony and child support based on their prior incomes.

A Man's Guide to Child Custody

Which usually means they can't reduce the amount of work they do, to create that income, so they do not have the time to spend with their children.

In two income families where mother and father both work outside the home, the reason that fathers again lose physical custody is because they generally have moved out, in order to cause the least disruption to the children. In doing so, they have created a family structure that a court will not change unless it is shown that mom is unstable or a bad parent, or some other change of circumstance that is significant.

Visitation

Reasonable visitation is due to every parent. What this means for the non-custodial parent is that they will have some amount of time given to them to be with their children, usually it is every other weekend and a weeknight dinner. This was decided many years ago as a "workable" situation and has become a default for the courts. It does not have to be that way, but if you and your ex cannot agree on a different arrangement. it is the most likely scenario.

Paternity Defined

Paternity actions decide that there is a legal relationship between a child and a man. They can be filed by either the mother or the father to determine and establish rights and responsibilities in regards to a child.

Traditionally they were filed by women seeking child support from a man for the child.

A Man's Guide to Child Custody

As society has changed and more people are having children outside of marriage, men are starting to file paternity actions to secure their rights to their children. As more and more men become primary caregivers, and it becomes more commonplace for a man to raise a child, these types of cases are becoming everyday occurrences.

If there is a question as to the actual paternity, a genetic test can be ordered and performed that will provide the court with 99% certainty as to whether a particular man is or is not the father of a child.

Rights of Unmarried Parents

Unmarried parents of a child are in a different legal position than married couples. The mother is automatically granted Legal and Physical Custody of a child upon birth because

A Man's Guide to Child Custody

it is clear that she is the mother.

An unmarried father, has to assert his rights, because it is not immediately clear that he is the father. Once a child is born, if he is certain that he is the father, he can sign the birth certificate and the Voluntary Declaration of Paternity which will act as a judgment of paternity within 60 days if he does not revoke it. When those two items are signed and recorded he becomes the father legally and will have a legal right to both Legal Custody and Physical Custody.

Just because he has the right to both Legal Custody and Physical Custody does not mean that they will be enforced automatically. That is why he must file a paternity action. By filing an action and receiving a court order, he can then enforce his visitation and legal rights to

A Man's Guide to Child Custody

a child's information.

Child Visitation

Reasonable visitation is due to every parent, for the non-custodial parent (usually the father) that means they must either have an arrangement with the mother, or ask a court to make visitation orders..

Most holidays will be shared, either by alternating them, where one parent takes the odd years and the other parent takes the even years, or the day is split with morning and afternoon sessions. Some holidays and special days are automatically given to you, as a father you can expect that visitation on Father's day will be yours as well as your birthday. The child's birthday will generally alternate from year to year.

A Man's Guide to Child Custody

Supervised Visitation

Supervised visitation is ordered when one parent asks for it, and the court believes that the other parent is dangerous, unstable, or requires supervision to ensure the child's safety. This is a standard request in Domestic Violence Restraining Orders, and it is regularly granted.

Monitoring can be done by either a professional, or a family member, or friend approved of, by the requesting party. The other parent is NOT an acceptable monitor. Professional monitors can be beneficial for the parent who is being supervised, as the professional can provide unbiased notes and reports to the court.

Many men think that supervision is humiliating. It is viewed by them as demeaning, belittling, and shameful. These feelings are

A Man's Guide to Child Custody

understandable, but the request for supervision is really more of a comment on the mother's state of mind, than it is the danger that the father presents.

Properly used, the fact that there is an objective third person to report to the court, can be useful, if the reports come back showing how devoted, attentive, and wonderful a father the man is, and how paranoid, overly protective and alienating the mother is.

Children of Domestic Partnerships

Children born during a Domestic Partnership are entitled to the same protections and rights as children born during a marriage. There are some technical issues regarding adoption by the non-biological parent and how that will affect a visitation and child custody plan.

A Man's Guide to Child Custody

Children's Preferences in Custody Disputes

In general a child is not expected, and frequently not allowed, to communicate what their preferences for custody are. The reason for this is to prevent one parent from trying to lobby for custody over the other parent. Many judges will not read letters from the child, no matter how old they are, as a matter of policy. The reason is to prevent the children from being put in the middle of the parent's dispute.

However, some judges will read a letter from a child, if they are old enough and if the judge feels that it was not a coerced letter. In California, a child may be emancipated at the age of 12, consequently some judges will use that as a starting age from which they will start to get information from the child.

A Man's Guide to Child Custody

Creative Child Custody Agreements

There are no real limits on what you and the other parent can come up with in terms of child custody. It is very dependent on your ability to work together. We have clients who alternate the child every week, others do every other day, some do living situations where the children stay in the house and the parents are the ones who rotate in and out of the house.

It is all a matter of negotiation, so long as you stay away from the judge.

Details on Visitation

Visitation is crucial for your relationship with your children. If you are the non-custodial parent, meaning you do not have the children the majority of the time, you need to A) be sure to use all the visitation time you were given either by the judge or in your agreement, and B)

A Man's Guide to Child Custody

keep a record of what you use, and how you use it.

The value of a Dad's Diary is crucial if you ever get into a fight with your ex over how much you really see your children. Frequently Moms like to say that "he never uses the time he's got" as a way to increase their child support. If you need to prove that you actually saw your child you must have a record of what you did, on what day, and be able to show the judge and your lawyer something to support your claims.

Developing a custody plan

The hardest part for most fathers is the realization that their career obligations interfere with the custody that they would like to have with their children. The reality is that a custody plan has to take into account the actual schedule of a child, the work schedule of both parents, and the current living situation.

If the family is still living under one roof, there is still time to plan and work out a schedule that will be equitable to the father's, and children's, advantage. If dad has already moved out, or been kicked out of the family home, it is going to be very hard to change that custody arrangement.

Special Needs Children

Special needs children require a much more thorough custody plan and depending on the severity of their needs, support from the parents may continue past the age of majority, when most support ends.

School plans and housing can be difficult to deal with when the parents have a special

A Man's Guide to Child Custody

needs child and are not agreeing on what is in the best interests of the child. This may lead to the request by one or both parents for a 730 Evaluation.

730 Evaluations of Custody

California Evidence Code §730 allows a court to appoint an expert to give the court additional information and an outside, objective determination of what is happening when the court has either conflicting testimony between the parties, or the situation is such that additional information would help the judge make a ruling.

A 730 Evaluation is usually a long, difficult, and emotional process that involves the family being interviewed by a psychologist over several sessions, both individually and in group settings. At the end of the evaluation process a report is generated by the psychologist or social worker for the court to review along with recommendations of what the custody should be.

Properly handled, a 730 Evaluation can be a huge benefit for a father who is fighting false charges or has an ex who is highly volatile and making co-parenting difficult. If a good expert is hired, one who is highly experienced and has great skill at determining when someone is lying, then the evaluation can be very beneficial.

These are not inexpensive. A 730 Evaluation can cost from $5,000 and there is no upper limit on what can be spent, though generally they come in between $5,000 and $10,000.

A Man's Guide to Child Custody

Out-of-State Custody Proceedings

If you have a custody determination in one state, and live in another, you should either arrange to have the case transferred to the new jurisdiction or be prepared to have the custody hearings held in the original state. The out of state rulings can be enforced in the state you and or the children live.

This is particularly true when it comes to the enforcement of Child Support Awards. The law allows for a Los Angeles Court through the District Attorney's office to enforce a judgment from Arizona when it comes to the collection of Child Support. But it will NOT hear or do anything about the custody and visitation, if you want to change that and get more time with your children.

A Man's Guide to Child Custody

Parental Alienation

Parental Alienation is a heartbreaking situation. When one parent, (usually an angry mother) attempts to cut the other parent out of the child's life by subtly and sometimes not so subtly alienating the affections of the child for the targeted parent. This is a very difficult situation to prove to a court, because the alienation is frequently masked to look like a) protection by the alienator, b) miscommunications, c) the targeted parent is being difficult, d) overreaction by the targeted parent and frequently there are "innocent" explanations for everything.

There is much controversy over whether or not it even exists. The American Psychological Association is reviewing the data, and is expected to decide that in the upcoming Diagnostic and Statistical Manual (DSM V) if

A Man's Guide to Child Custody

there will be a test to determine if a parent is either the perpetrator or victim of Parental Alienation. However, at this time it is not a recognized diagnosis by the medical establishment.

We have fought these cases, and won, but they are expensive, emotionally draining, time consuming cases because of their subtlety.

Parental Alienation frequently hides behind a mask of "concerned parent" but its effect is to make the child feel unsafe around the alienated parent – which is child abuse.

Here is just one example of Parental Alienation and how it can look like Mom is just being concerned: "Janey, remember, when you're at Daddy's you can always call me and I'll come get you if you don't feel good." That is setting Mom up as a rescuer, and implying that

A Man's Guide to Child Custody

Dad's house is not safe for Janey to be sick in. It paints Dad as less than a good parent by showing Janey that Mom has to always be ready to come and pick up the pieces when Dad fails.

Stepped-Up Visitation

The development of a child from a vulnerable, totally dependent newborn to an independent teen, requires varying degrees of visitation time with the father. While the baby is breastfeeding the father is not considered an essential part of the child's life. Once the child reaches the point of eating food, the father can take a more active role in the development of the child.

Fathers who want to be an active part in their child's lives will find that they can receive more and more visitation, up to a 50% split, if they have the availability, but it will come in a

A Man's Guide to Child Custody

stepped up fashion. If the parents do not live together, a newborn's father may have only a 4-hour visit on a Saturday, then more time, then overnights, then blocks of days.

This same concept of stepped up visitation also applies to fathers who have been absent from a child's life and want to reunite. If a child does not have an established relationship with the father, the court will require a "Reunification Plan" that uses greater and greater blocks of time to allow a child to adjust to the new relationship with a parent they didn't know.

Understanding Child Custody Laws

Child custody law and decisions are the most difficult to explain to people who don't eat, live, and breathe them. They are heartbreaking decisions by someone who

A Man's Guide to Child Custody

doesn't have to live with the results. They are made by judges who have limited information and in most cases are overworked and trying to do what is best for a child that they don't know personally.

Child custody battles are hard fought and usually have no winners. The cases turn on a few facts and what looks like a slam dunk case can turn out to be a dead bang loser with just one or two facts perceived differently.

In some areas of the law, like criminal, there are clear, black and white rules. In Family Law, and in Child Custody in particular, everything is a constantly evolving shade of grey.

For example, when a court looks at a parent who chronically abuses alcohol, but has no criminal record such as a DUI, that fact may

A Man's Guide to Child Custody

carry little weight. But another parent who occasionally smokes marijuana could be put through a series of supervised visitations based solely on the request of the other parent who provides a declaration that there is marijuana smoking going on.

Uniform Child Custody Jurisdiction Act

The Uniform Child Custody Jurisdiction and Enforcement Act (UCCJEA) is what determines whether or not a particular state can hear a case involving a child, based on where that child has lived just prior to the filing of the case.

The UCCJEA allows for a state to take Temporary Jurisdiction over a child if there is an allegation of child abuse or domestic violence, otherwise the court must defer to the appropriate court. This is a highly technical area

A Man's Guide to Child Custody

of the law, and most people are not qualified to interpret it without an attorney.

Parenting Plans

Parenting plans are those agreements made between the parents in regards to child custody, child visitation, holidays, schooling, religious training, extra-curricular activities, and all other aspects of raising a child.

Court ordered mediation is usually the place where parenting plans first get negotiated, if the parties can agree on some or all of the topics, the parenting plan will be written up and then entered as a judgment that will become enforceable by the court and the police.

A Man's Guide to Child Custody

Move-Away Orders

Move-Away cases are heartbreaking. When one parent has a desire to move, and they have custody of a child, they need to file a motion with the court to get permission to move the child's residence, unless the other parent will agree in writing to a modification.

The usual reason for these move aways is the need for work, or a new relationship. In either case, a court cannot restrain the parent from moving, they have a Constitutional right to move, the court can however restrain the child from being moved, and that is why a court order is needed.

Once a motion is filed, the court will order an evaluation of the custody, this can be either a short or "fast track" evaluation, which is only a few hours, or a full 730 Evaluation of

A Man's Guide to Child Custody

what is best for the child, if the parents have the money to fund the battle and the evaluation.

In the "up is down, and black is white" world of child custody, the better the parent's relationship is, in terms of working with each other for child custody, the more likely it is the court will allow the child to move. The reasoning here is that the moving parent will continue to work with the non-moving parent and help the relationship between the child and staying parent.

Additionally, if there are siblings involved the move is more likely to be granted as courts will almost never split up the children, even if they are only half-siblings.

Move-Away or Relocation Situations

Move-Away or Relocation situations

A Man's Guide to Child Custody

usually involve Mom wanting to move for a better job or a new boyfriend. Sometimes they are used by Mom as a way to increase the parental alienation of the father, and are masked with the "new job" or "new boyfriend" cover. Courts will almost always grant these move-away requests, though they can put some serious restrictions and requirements in place.

Frequently the staying behind parent can have large blocks of time with the child, such as all the spring, winter and summer vacations. Or the moving parent may have to bear the burden of most of the traveling costs.

Every situation presents different obstacles and opportunities in move away cases. There are a many factors that go into whether the judge will allow the move away to happen, but generally the judge's job is to make sure that

A Man's Guide to Child Custody

visitation will continue, because in the end, the moving parent has a constitutional right to move.

This is why you should always meet with an experienced attorney to discuss your options.

Chapter 4 - Child Support Strategy

Many men think they can simply stop working. That won't work. The courts will impute your income. Which means they will assume you are capable of making a certain amount of money. This can be very expensive because judges have wide discretion based on your past history of saying what you are capable of earning today.

Underperforming at work

Many paying fathers think that they can avoid paying Child Support by underperforming at work. This is a mistake and can result in a

A Man's Guide to Child Custody

court ordering an amount that is based upon historical performance. If a top salesperson who normally makes $200,000 a year, suddenly is making only $20,000 a year, and tries to lower their support, the court will want to know why the sudden drop in income. If there is a verifiable outside reason, like the salesperson sold a product that was then outlawed, this is believable and a court MAY reduce the award based on the change in circumstances.

However, if the salesperson was an advertising sales rep for the Los Angeles Times and they haven't lost their job, the court may look at the situation and decide that the paying father is underperforming at work, deliberately not working up to their potential, so that they can lower their payments. If a court decides that the loss of income is intentional, they may refuse to lower the child support.

A Man's Guide to Child Custody

Vocational Testing

People will occasionally claim that they cannot work and should not have to pay. This will also happen in child support cases, where one party will say that they have no skills, or no jobs are available for them and that is why the child support should be increased.

In all cases where an ex is under an obligation to be self-supporting, and this is most of them, if they are not working, or they are claiming that they cannot work or cannot find a job, we can ask the court to order that they be tested for vocational abilities. This is a skills test to see what jobs they are suited to perform. Most people can do more than one job, and a vocational test will allow for an objective third party to make a determination as to what type of work a person is capable of performing. Once we've found out that a person has greater

A Man's Guide to Child Custody

vocational skills, it makes the argument that they can't find work, harder for them to maintain.

If we find out that a person has a college degree in accounting, then there is no reason they can't find work as a bookkeeper, accounting clerk, warehouse manager, inventory clerk, or a host of other jobs. By then showing the judge that there are those jobs available, the judge can then impute income, AS IF they had that job. A judge cannot make someone get job, but a judge can treat them as if they had the income from the work.

Child Support

Child support is money that is paid to contribute to the expenses necessary for the maintenance and upbringing of a child. It is based on many factors - the time that the parents share the child, the income levels of each

A Man's Guide to Child Custody

parent, the age of the child, the number of children involved, other children from other relationships, etc.

Child support can be decided between mother and father on a very casual basis and the court need not be involved, or it can be a very specific, hard fought battle involving wage garnishments, vocational testing of parents to determine if they are underperforming, and asset searches to determine if money is being hidden.

The hard part for men to accept is that while their finances and lifestyle are open to exploration and examination by the courts, how the money is spent by Mom is completely untouchable. The court will not consider what Mom is doing with the money, whether it goes for facials or food is not the court's concern. Men cannot make Mom do an accounting, but

A Man's Guide to Child Custody

Mom can make Dad do an accounting to prove that he is paying his child support, and that he is paying the correct child support amount.

Child Support Defense

Child support is a fact of life for fathers, but that doesn't mean that it should be a blank check for mothers. Which is why it is so important for a man to appear and defend himself in a child support case.

The mother of a child can file an action for child support and she can claim that the father makes $10,000 a month, and if he doesn't appear in court to defend that, the judge may make a child support order based on mom's statements, which are under penalty of perjury.

It is crucial that a man defend himself in a child support case. It is also crucial that child

A Man's Guide to Child Custody

custody and visitation be addressed to make sure that dad is getting as much visitation as possible with his child, as that will affect how much support is awarded to mom. You cannot change visitation in a District Attorney's Child Support Case, so be sure that a paternity case is opened and that an Order To Show Cause hearing is filed every time that Mom wants to increase the child support.

Child Support Enforcement – Wage Garnishments

Enforcement of a child support award can be done casually between the parties, where Dad writes a check each week or month. It is absolutely essential, that Dad write a check or make an electronic transfer to Mom. Never use cash. EVER. Dads have to be able to prove that they have paid their child support, otherwise they may end up having to pay it

A Man's Guide to Child Custody

twice.

When you come to a lawyer's office and say, "I paid my child support." The first question asked will be "How?" It is recommended that you always have a means of proof available.

If you fall behind on your payments of child support, your driver's license, realtors license, or other professional license can be suspended until you get current or make a repayment plan.

Wage Garnishments are another area where men feel humiliated, embarrassed, shameful and guilty about their child support. This is understandable, but it is not a condemnation of them as men, in fact, it makes it much easier to prove that you have paid your child support, and that you are a stand-up father who IS paying his child support. Rather than fight the garnishment, most men should embrace it as a way of proving to the court and to the world that they are taking their responsibility seriously. Plus, it's one less check you have to write, and really, do you want to be writing her a check each month?

Child Support Guidelines

The guideline support is based on a formula that is so complex only a computer can determine what is the right number. However, the rule of thumb is 25% of your GROSS income as a guesstimate of the amount of child support you will pay.

There are online sources for you to figure out what you think it will be, but the best way is to meet with an attorney who has the Dissomaster program in California, or your state.

A Man's Guide to Child Custody

Child Support Modifications

Child Support is always modifiable, and that means that if you get a promotion your ex can file a motion to have the child support increased. It also means that if you lose your job you need to file a motion immediately to have your support reduced based on your new circumstances.

Generally if nothing changes, a court will not modify your child support, but you can be brought in every six months to confirm that you are paying the correct amount of money.

Department of Child Support Services

In Los Angeles, and throughout California, the Department of Child Support Services handles the enforcement of child support if the mother has opened a case with them. That means that they will place a wage

A Man's Guide to Child Custody

garnishment on you, and can take your tax return if there is an unpaid child support amount.

The Department of Child Support Services website has a child support calculator that you can use to determine what the state guidelines are for you, based on your income level and the amount of visitation you have with your child.

Dissomaster Child Support Calculator

The Child Support guideline is based on a complex algebraic formula that is so difficult only a computer can determine it. However, we use the rule of thumb of 25% of your GROSS income for what your child support will be, if you have one child, and the standard "Dad Package" of visitation – every other weekend and a mid-week dinner, which is about 20% of

A Man's Guide to Child Custody

custodial time.

The proprietary computer program that we use is called Dissomaster. You can go to your state's Department of Child Support Services website where they will usually have a program that is used by the courts to determine the child support they will order you to pay.

High-Earner Child Support

Child support is supposed to maintain a child in fairly even living environments. The reason for this is that the courts don't want one parent, who may earn substantially more than the other parent, to try to "win" the love and affection of the child by buying toys and other gifts.

This means that the court will look to both parties incomes to make a child support award based on what is needed to equalize the living environments. What this means is that if one parent is a high earner and the other parent is an average earner, the court may deviate from the Guideline support awards and award a sum of money that is much higher than the computer program would come up with. Or it may reduce the amount that the Guideline support would be if there are factors that would result in an absurd amount of money being paid.

How to Calculate a Child Support

Calculating Child support takes a highly complex computer program, and even then, sometimes the court will ignore the results if they are deemed unfair, or are overly generous. This is another one of the many gray areas in family law, the Guideline Child Support awards are a starting point, but if your situation is

A Man's Guide to Child Custody

different for some reason you should speak to an attorney to determine what is the most realistic result.

New Mate Income

In some cases, though not most, a new spouse's income can be used as a factor in child support calculations, but generally, the courts only want to know what the actual parent's income is in determining the support award.

If there is a special needs child involved, the new spouse's income may be a factor, particularly if the primary custodial parent cannot work while caring for the special needs child.

A Man's Guide to Child Custody

Chapter 5 – Case Studies

CHILD SUPPORT AND VISITATION - Greg B.

We represented the man in this case against an ex-wife who wanted to prevent him from seeing his son, so that she could receive an increased Child Support award. We were victorious in not only keeping his support low, but increasing his visitation with his son through the crucial pre-teen years.

A Man's Guide to Child Custody

DISTRICT ATTORNEY CHILD SUPPORT COLLECTION ABUSE - Curtis M.

We represented our client against the District Attorney's office for a back child support collection matter in which he had fully paid all of his support, but the DA's office continued to collect surplus funds that the ex was no longer entitled to.

PARENTAL ALIENATION - CHILD ABUSE - John B.

For this father, we had to fight to prove that the mother was not only an unfit mother, but that she was physically abusing their daughters, engaging in extensive parental alienation, and emotionally abusing the children.

It took a lot of work, and after several

A Man's Guide to Child Custody

hearings (Orders to Show Cause - "OSCs") we were able to make the judge see that the father was the more stable, loving and attentive environment for the children to be living in.

PARENTAL ALIENATION - CHILD SEXUAL ABUSE ALLEGATIONS AGAINST FATHER - Doug G.

For this super devoted dad, we had to fight to prove that the mothers multiple allegations of sexual molestation were false. By agreeing to a full psychological evaluation (Family Code §730) we were able to provide the court with an outside, independent, unbiased opinion of the father's fitness.

The court agreed, and said that if Mom decides to "move away" from the state of California, the child's primary custody would transfer to father. This was a major win for this devoted dad who loves his child.

INTERNATIONAL CHILD CUSTODY DISPUTE THE HAGUE CONVENTION - Henry W.

For this father, we continued to fight to show that the mother was not only unfit, due to her chemical dependency issues, but as she was living in another country, could not provide for regular and ongoing visitation.

CHILD ABANDONMENT BY MOTHER, CUSTODY FIGHT - Raul C.

Representing the father, who had full custody of his son after mom abandoned him, we protected his rights and secured a custody plan that allowed his son the continued, stable, secure home life that he enjoyed with his father. Mom was allowed only a visitation schedule.

A Man's Guide to Child Custody

CHILD SUPPORT MODIFICATION - John W.

A short term relationship, became a 19 year drama for this man who fathered children that mom was using to extract child support. We held the line on keeping the support amounts low and in line with what the children really needed.

PATERNITY DEFENSE - John Q.

This alleged father came to us after he was served with paperwork demanding that he start paying child support. He claimed that the kids weren't his, so we defended. The initial DNA tests results showed it was not his kid.

A Man's Guide to Child Custody

CHILD SUPPORT - DRIVER'S LICENSE RELEASE - Frank S.

Dad had fallen behind on his child support payments, so the Department of Motor Vehicles, at the request of the Department of Child Support Services suspended his driving privileges. This prevented him from working so that he could make the money, to pay his child support. We appeared in court and were able to work out a release of the driver's license and a reasonable payment plan that allowed dad to get back on track.

CHILD SUPPORT ABUSE BY DISTRICT ATTORNEY - Cal P.

Another loving father who fell behind on his child support payments. His records were not clean and orderly and we had to do a full accounting going back years to find that he had actually overpaid. It was long battle with the District Attorney, Child Support Services, and a vindictive, greedy mom - but we won.

OVERREACHING BY DISTRICT ATTORNEY FOR BACK CHILD SUPPORT - Keith A.

In yet another horror story about the District Attorney's Office and the Child Support Service's incompetence, this dad, who made all of his child support payments, had his tax refunds, and bank accounts garnished by child support authorities when they "mistakenly" erased all of his payments. They took $25,000 of his money, not once, but TWICE, because of their errors.

It took several hearings and full accountings, but eventually we were able to get

A Man's Guide to Child Custody

all of the money returned and the matter cleared up.

Chapter 6

Essays for Fathers

A Man's Guide to Child Custody

A Man's Guide to Child Custody

THE THREE P's OF CHILD CUSTODY FOR FATHERS

I believe that parents should be forced to take an equal division of time in their children's care. Fathers should be required by law to take their children 50% of the time.

Mothers frequently withhold their children from the fathers based on the false perception that they are not nurturing enough. Courts tend to support this canard and the only way we will be able to change it is by men fighting for custody. It is happening more often and as the studies are beginning to show, men are just as capable of being loving and nurturing parents as women. They simply have been

A Man's Guide to Child Custody

denied the opportunity for too long. It's the same argument that feminists made when it came to the workplace and equal pay.

The alienating behavior is commonly masked as mom being "protective" – it's bunk. We see this type of controlling behavior all too often in our practice, and it is a detriment to the father/child bonding.

It is understandable that when a child is young, they may need the mother for breastfeeding. But that is no excuse for a father to be denied solo parenting time. Frequently the mom claims that the father is not a good parent, or too immature, or too uneducated to provide for a newborn. I think those are weak arguments at best and disingenuous at worst. If a man is old enough to father a child, and to be required to

A Man's Guide to Child Custody

pay child support, then he should be old enough to take up the mantel of parenting.

Today, as it stands, fathers who want to obtain, or increase, their visitation and custody orders need to keep in mind the following: **Proximity, Paperwork and Persistence.** The Three Ps can make or break your chances of getting the orders issued by the judge. Most fathers start out a custody case at a disadvantage. When dad moves out, the children are left with mom, and that becomes the way the court is inclined to keep the situation. The moment that dad moves out of the family home is the moment that mom gains an advantage in child custody hearings.

Here's why - the courts don't want to upset the children's living environment. They

A Man's Guide to Child Custody

focus on keeping the child stable, and that means in their historical home.

So how then does a man recover from the mistake of moving out of the house? He must show to the court that he can effectively parent the child, with as little disruption to the child's routine as possible.

PROXIMITY

This means how far or close dad lives to the child's home and school. This is a major factor in increasing, or acquiring custody and visitation. The closer dad is to the home and school, the more easily he can be present for the child, and the courts give this great weight. If the choice is for a child to be in a car for 5 minutes getting from mom's home to school or a 25-minute drive from dad's home, the court is

A Man's Guide to Child Custody

going to prefer mom's home. It is also more likely that the child's friends and social network are close to the school they attend, which is a factor for the court.

PAPERWORK

Cases are won or lost on documentation. Dads should keep a calendar or a diary of all the time that they are with their child. In any contested case, mom has something that she will use to show the court how little time dad spends with the kids.

A simple calendar which shows the days that dad took his child, and what they did on those days can make all the difference for a change in custody. If dad keeps the receipts for what he did with his child, it will allow his lawyer to prove that he took the child to see the

A Man's Guide to Child Custody

movie "Cars" on a day when mom says he didn't visit. This is a crucial credibility issue, and one that with a little bit of work by dad, can yield big gains. The court will see that dad is truthful, which goes a long way towards winning the credibility wars, which in turn can lead to more time with his child.

PERSISTENCE

The biggest factor that affects whether or not a dad will win more visitation or even equal custody, is his ability to come back, time and time again. The successful dad in family court, is the dad who never gave up, and was willing to do whatever it took, no matter how difficult it was, or how long it took, to prove to the court that he wanted and was capable of being a loving, attentive, and present father.

A Man's Guide to Child Custody

The successful dad who wants to increase his custody and visitation, will live close to his child, keep good records, and never give up when dealt a bad hand.

Society is changing, and as more men take up the duties of being a responsible parent, it will become easier for all fathers to have the custodial time and visitation they want with their children.

A Man's Guide to Child Custody

A Man's Guide to Child Custody

FATHERS SHOULD NOT LEAVE THE FAMILY HOME

I am asked frequently about the issue of whether or not fathers should leave the family home. Doing so is a big mistake in child custody cases. It sets the mother up as the de facto Primary Custodian, which is why most men never get the custody that they so desperately want. Child Custody battles are largely fought and won LONG before the court even looks at the case.

Sitting before me is a man, a father, a provider of love to his children. He has soothed scraped knees, taught bike riding, and changed wet bed sheets at 3 a.m. He is fighting back tears because we are not close enough yet for him to let me see the hurt. I know he needs to let the pain out, I know how to say just the right

A Man's Guide to Child Custody

thing to make him feel comfortable, and his defenses crumble. For the first time in two months, he allows himself to feel the loss of his family.

I'm a divorce attorney. I'm one of those people that helps others through an incredibly difficult period of their life. I have to deliver bad news regularly. Some days it feels like that's all I do. I specialize in helping men; fathers and husbands who are entering a minefield, financially and emotionally, through what is arguably one of the most difficult and treacherous periods of their life.

Frequently a man comes to my office having already left the family home and the first thing he says is, "I don't care about the house, I just want to see my kids." What he doesn't

A Man's Guide to Child Custody

know, and what I have to tell him, is that he has already lost the war for custody.

He and his wife were not getting along, they were bickering and fighting in front of the kids, she kept telling him to "get out, just leave!" He thought it was best for the kids — that if he moved out the fighting would stop.

Big mistake. Huge. Tremendously bad move.

The only time that I tell a man to leave the home is if there is physical violence, or she's deceitful enough to lie about being abused to get a restraining order. Other than that, moving out is the single worst thing a man can do in a divorce, financially, and emotionally. If he moves out, he will have to get an apartment, which takes more money. It increases the financial strain on the couple, who are already

A Man's Guide to Child Custody

low on money. He now may have to buy furnishings, dishes, pots and pans, etc. for his apartment. Plus anything the kids need is now duplicated. As the money gets tighter, the fighting will intensify and if he's not living with the family, soon enough she'll be after him for child support, which will only put more strain on him.

When he moves out, the little communication that was happening between him and her usually gets worse. Frequently it stops altogether, and the reasons for the breakup never get talked about, or worse, he now gets blamed for "leaving." This often makes him feel guilty, trapped in a "Catch-22" situation and he just wants to give up and run away.

Lastly, and the worst part of this tragedy, is that moving out has created a "status quo" as

A Man's Guide to Child Custody

far as the courts are concerned in regards to the children. Since dad left the kids with mom, the court thinks that they should be with her, and that's what is most likely going to happen. He will see them every other weekend and a weeknight dinner. This is the bad news I have to deliver to the man who sits in front of me in tears.

He didn't know that was going to happen. He didn't think he'd lose seeing his kids all the time. He doesn't care about the house, the furniture, the only thing he wants is to be a dad, and now he's a weekend dad. All it took was for her to push him out of the house.

Simply because he left, he's now a part-time parent. He did it to create peace, which didn't happen. He did it to make his relationship with his kids better — that certainly won't

A Man's Guide to Child Custody

happen. He did it because he thought he'd get a 50/50 custody deal, which is a pipe dream, while her child support is tied to how much time she has the kids versus him.

Men are mostly ignorant about what happens in a divorce or a child custody battle. Men don't talk about it with each other. Men don't share how to plot, strategize and set up the situation to our advantage, which leads to their undoing.

Fathers shouldn't leave until they absolutely have to. Fathers need to talk to each other to find out what to do. Men use coaches in sports, and mentors in business and they need to rely on each other to get through life's challenges, and to keep what is theirs: their children.

A Man's Guide to Child Custody

FATHER'S DAY SPECIAL: ON FATHERHOOD AND RAISING MEN

I never really knew my father. Well, let me be clearer. I know who he was, he lived with me until I was 12, and then I lived with him on summer vacations and such. I have memories of going fishing once or twice with him. I recall fighting with him as a teenager, and the weekend before he died we had a great conversation, but I was 19 and in Boston for the summer.

My father was a World War 2 vet, but the way he told it, he was on an island in the pacific resupplying ships and it was a blast. He went to college on the GI bill and was a salesman. He sold printing presses, then life insurance, and then funeral plans.

A Man's Guide to Child Custody

He was the 13th child born and the 11th child to live in his family. He was the baby who was raised by his sisters. Which partly explains his life skills, or lack thereof. Alcoholism took a hold of him fiercely, and it effected my family dramatically.

I am the baby in my family. I was the third son born, my parents were in their mid 40's and by the time I came along, alcoholism was in full bloom and its effects were being felt throughout the family. My parents fought bitterly and viciously. My brothers, who were 16 and 14 years older than me, had more fully seen the terrors that I felt the repercussions of as a child.

So when my parents finally divorced, it brought peace to the household, but there was a cost. My father became sober soon afterwards, but I was a pre-teen, and parenting a pre-teen

A Man's Guide to Child Custody

from afar is nigh on impossible. The job fell to my older brother Chris.

He was an island of calm, mostly, in a household of alcoholism and anxiety. For even though my parents had divorced, the long term negative effects of their marriage remained. My mother was struggling to make it financially, and battling with the bottle herself. My brother Chris took up the responsibility for being a father figure in my life and though he did a great job, and I love and respect him for it, he was only 28, and he had my father as his father. He was denied a good father just as much as I was, probably more.

When I look at my father's life, I see the pattern of my life. I see how he was raised by his siblings, I see the lack of strong male figures to teach the hard lessons in life.

A Man's Guide to Child Custody

It is perhaps one of the reasons why I am attracted to the work I do.

As much as a mother can nurture a child, she cannot teach a boy how to be a man. Young boys need their mothers, but the more I think about it, and the more I learn about the way men develop, I believe it is the men who teach boys how to be men.

In the ancient Grecian state of Sparta, boys were raised by their mothers until they were 7 when there were sent to be raised by men. The understanding of boys and men, the ways in which we think and act, versus the manner in which we should act, these are lessons that need to be taught by men because we speak a common language.

Only another man intuitively understands my impulses towards anger, aggression, and sex.

A Man's Guide to Child Custody

Only older, wiser men have been able to show me a better way of dealing with those issues.

Fathers, and father figures, are vitally important to the upbringing of boys. It is a crime in our country that so many men are sidelined by the courts, and their exes, when it comes to the raising of the children. It is the future men who are being denied vital life lessons, and it is our society that will pay the price.

The conventional wisdom that the mother is the better parent in all things is as absurd as hiring a plumber to fix a soufflé. Mothers are vitally important at certain times, just as fathers are vitally important at others, to idolize one, and ignore the other is philosophically imbalanced and illogical.

This Father's Day I'd like to see an awareness of the important role that men play in

A Man's Guide to Child Custody

raising boys, who in turn become fathers. Father's Day is a day honoring fathers and celebrating fatherhood, paternal bonds, and the influence of fathers in society, but to do that, we first have to really understand what they do. It's about more than just paying child support and every other weekend of visitation.

At least, it should be.

A Man's Guide to Child Custody

FATHERS SHOULD GET AN AUTOMATIC 50% CHILD CUSTODY

When a man is first told he is going to be a father, naturally the expectations of what the future will look like pop into his head. He may think of fishing trips and baseball games, ballet recitals and happy holiday memories being created.

At first he and mom are getting along great, they both agree on what needs to be done to properly raise a child. Mom's in charge a lot, at first, because of the necessity to breastfeed, attend to the endless needs of a newborn and her own maternal instincts. This works at first, but it also sets a pattern for dad's relationship with the child. Mom's in charge and dad does what mom says to provide for the growth and well-being of the newborn.

A Man's Guide to Child Custody

That pattern continues, and hopefully in healthy relationships the parties begin to equalize as the baby becomes a toddler and mom can back off and dad can take on a stronger role.

But not always. Sometimes, the relationship stays imbalanced, those are the ones I think I was seeing this weekend – the detached fathers who have stepped back from an active role in their family, and that's a shame. They should be contributing and directing the growth and setting the boundaries for their children as much as Mom, if not more.

Sometimes a divorce happens. Then the parties have to come up with a written agreement on how to parent their child. Most parents don't have too much conflict over this. Thanks to a common heritage, or at least a common set of desires, the Parenting Plan can

A Man's Guide to Child Custody

fairly easily be agreed to. Mom gets Mother's Day, Dad gets Father's day, they alternate the big holidays, etc.

Sometimes though, there is the Grand Battle Royale. Where one parent doesn't want to share the child. Usually it is mom, who is too attached to her child, and she feels that Dad is a bad influence, lacks parenting skills, is too indulgent, or too strict - "he never shows up on time, he never returns the child on time." And the most common complaint of all: "he has a new girlfriend who is inappropriate."

This is where the Parenting Plan becomes the roadmap of your relationship, not only with your child, but with your ex. The Parenting Plan will determine when you as a father have time with your child. If you have a cooperative ex, this can be a very flexible agreement, as simple as, "we'll share the kids", other times you need

A Man's Guide to Child Custody

to have an excruciatingly specific plan. This plan will determine how much, how long and how often you have to interact with your ex and your child. If she's still angry and bitter, the more specific the plan, the easier it will be to have a court, or the police enforce it, and that means fewer headaches for dad.

Married dads don't get to spend a lot of time with their kids, divorced dads get even less. There are few years in which a father has the opportunity to have any long lasting positive effect on his children, he should spend what few hours he has, really making a difference. That's why I think that more fathers should step up to the plate and take a stronger role in their children's life. It should be mandatory that if you divorce and have kids, you automatically have the kids 50% of the time.

A Man's Guide to Child Custody

That won't be popular among many divorced moms, partly because they are still angry, and for some, because they don't want to see a reduction in their child support. But the reality is that, as a society, we need to have more men, acting like men, and teaching their children what it means to be a man, and that includes their daughters. So that they know what to expect of their future spouses.

A Man's Guide to Child Custody

A Man's Guide to Child Custody

About the Author

David Pisarra has been practicing Family Law in the southern California counties of Los Angeles, Riverside, Orange, Ventura and San Diego for over 10 years. He has wide experience in Divorces, Child Support, Child Custody, Paternity, Alimony / Spousal Support, and Domestic Violence cases. He has represented both men and women, straight people and gay people successfully.

Mr. Pisarra has fought increases in Alimony, and also termination of Spousal Support orders. His firm believes that testing the supported spouse with vocational testing, is underused and that many paying spouses could reduce their alimony by finding out that the ex could work or has some responsibility to earn an income.

Mr. Pisarra has represented many fathers in paternity cases. Fathers have both rights and responsibilities to their children. Whether or not the child is planned, the dad has an obligation to be there for his children. It is always in the man's best interest to confirm that he is the father and if he is, to take responsibility and have an active role in the child's life.

A Man's Guide to Child Custody

www.ingramcontent.com/pod-product-compliance
Lightning Source LLC
Chambersburg PA
CBHW051454290426
44109CB00016B/1750